BEST
WORD BOOK
EVER

THE ALPHABET

The alligator is eating an apple.
The goose is wearing gloves.
What is the xiphias doing?

G goose

A alligator

B bear

H heart

C cat

I ice cream cone

D dog

J

jack-o'-lantern

E egg

K kangaroo

letter carrier

F fish

L

M mailbag

2

N nut

O owl

P present

Q queen

R rug

S spider

T turtle

U umbrella

V vase

W walrus

X xiphias

xylophone

Y yarn

Z zipper

mosquito

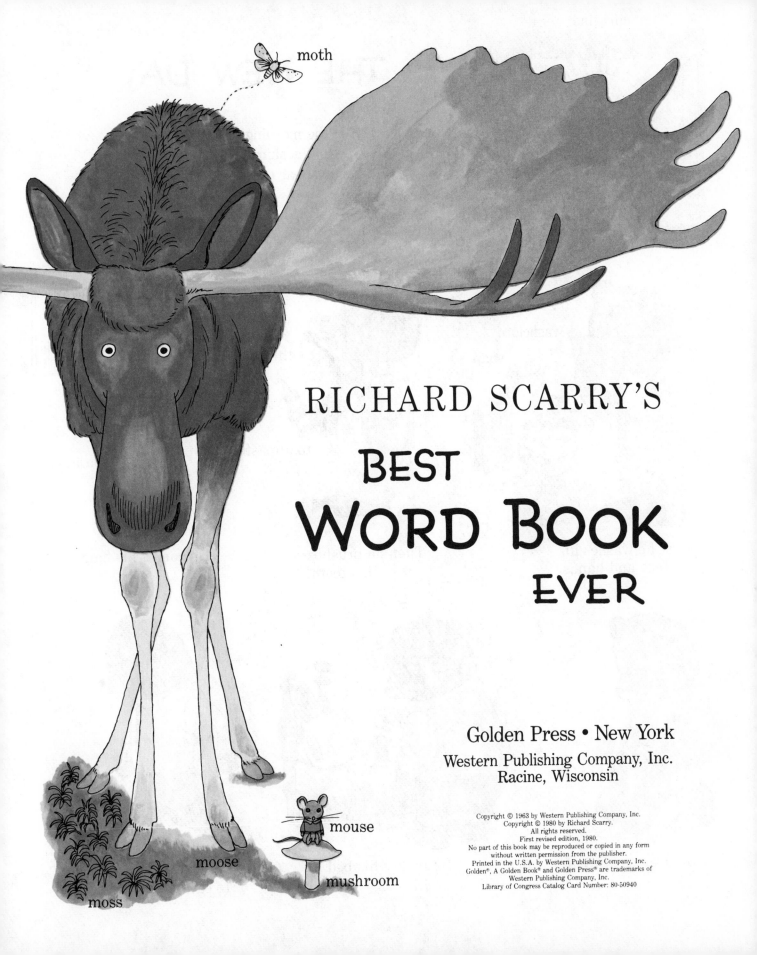

moth

RICHARD SCARRY'S
BEST
WORD BOOK
EVER

Golden Press • New York
Western Publishing Company, Inc.
Racine, Wisconsin

mouse

moose

mushroom

moss

THE NEW DAY

curtains

sun

window

It is the morning of a new day.
The sun is shining.
Kenny Bear gets up out of bed.

washcloth

soap

towel

First he washes his
face and hands.

toothbrush

toothpaste

Then he brushes
his teeth.

mirror

comb

pajamas

He combs his hair.

shirt

pants

He dresses himself.

He makes his bed.

He goes to the kitchen
to eat his breakfast.

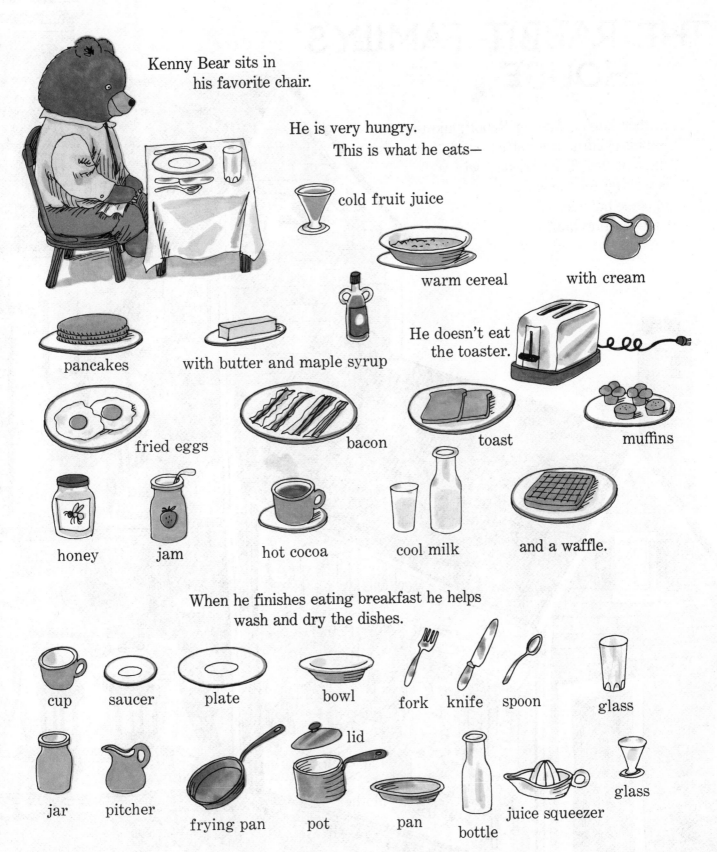

Kenny Bear sits in
his favorite chair.

He is very hungry.
This is what he eats—

cold fruit juice

warm cereal

with cream

He doesn't eat
the toaster.

pancakes

with butter and maple syrup

fried eggs

bacon

toast

muffins

honey

jam

hot cocoa

cool milk

and a waffle.

When he finishes eating breakfast he helps
wash and dry the dishes.

cup

saucer

plate

bowl

fork

knife

spoon

glass

jar

pitcher

frying pan

lid

pot

pan

bottle

juice squeezer

glass

Now he is ready to play with his friends.

7

THE RABBIT FAMILY'S HOUSE

Father Rabbit, Mother Rabbit, and the
Rabbit children are getting ready for
the new day. Their friend Owl
is waiting for the children
to come outside.
Can you find him?

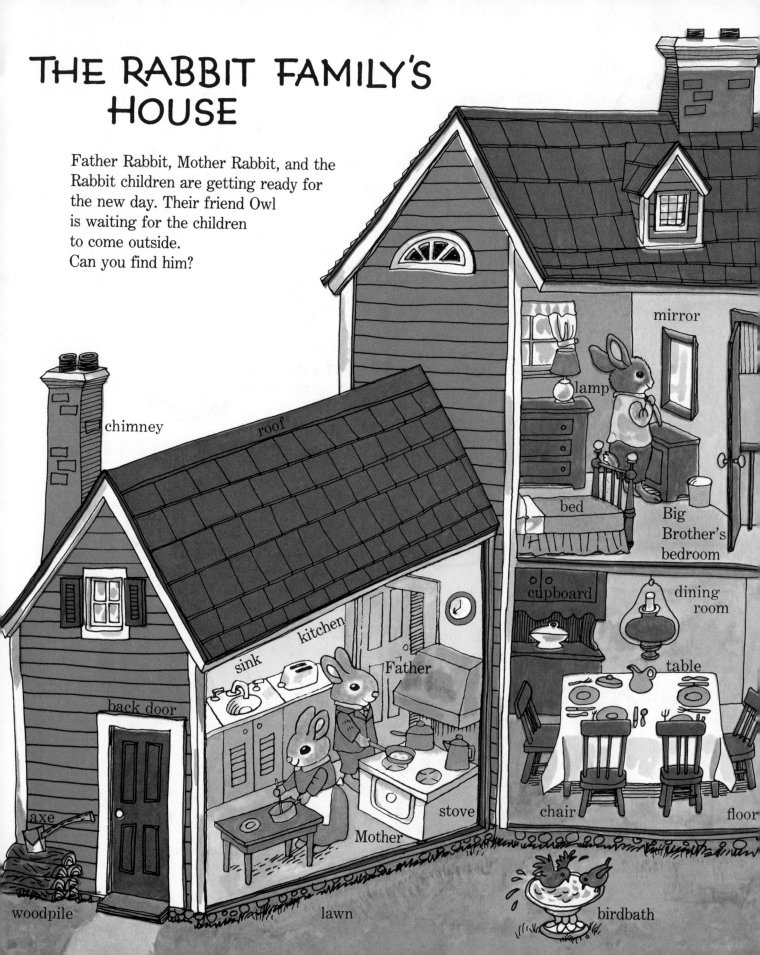

chimney

roof

mirror

lamp

bed

Big
Brother's
bedroom

cupboard

dining
room

table

sink

kitchen

Father

back door

chair

floor

axe

stove

Mother

woodpile

lawn

birdbath

WHOO

owl

smoke

antenna

light switch

television set

record player

hassock

Mickey

bunk bed

bathroom

Molly

upstairs hall

bedroom

front door

living room

candle

outside light

picture

telephone

fireplace

stairs

sofa or couch

front hall

doormat

rug

window

stone walk

9

PAINTING AND DRAWING WITH COLORS

Painting and drawing are fun.
You can use bright colors.
You can paint with brushes
or even your fingers. You can
draw with crayons or pencils.
What do you like to draw?

finger painting

paper

make orange

make green

pencil

eraser

pencil drawing

make violet

make pink

make gray

make brown

water dish

smock

poster paint

paintbrushes

crayons

watercolors

pastels

TOYS

Sometimes it is fun to play by yourself. Sometimes it is fun to play with your friends. What are your favorite toys? Do you like to play with blocks?

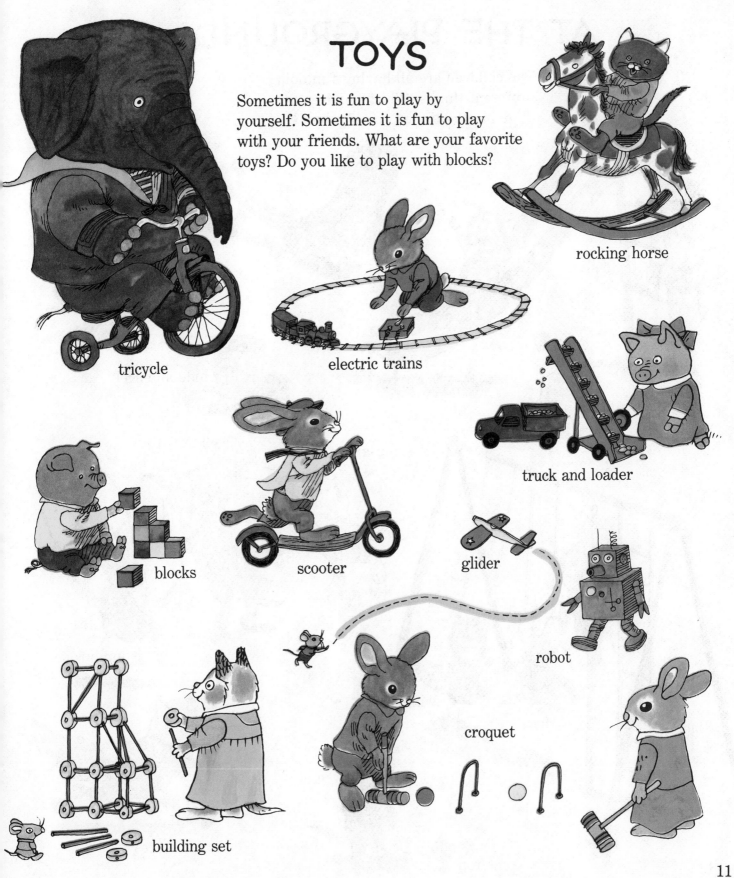

rocking horse

tricycle

electric trains

truck and loader

blocks

scooter

glider

robot

building set

croquet

AT THE PLAYGROUND

The children are all having fun doing different things. Which children are doing the things you like best?

seesaw

slide

leapfrog

hide-and-seek

somersault

ring-around-a-rosie

jump rope

ladder

rings

swing

sliding pole

roller skates

top

bubble blowing

kite

jungle gym

merry-go-round

tag

ring toss

hoop rolling

jacks

marbles

sandbox

kite string

bouncing ball

hopscotch

13

hammer

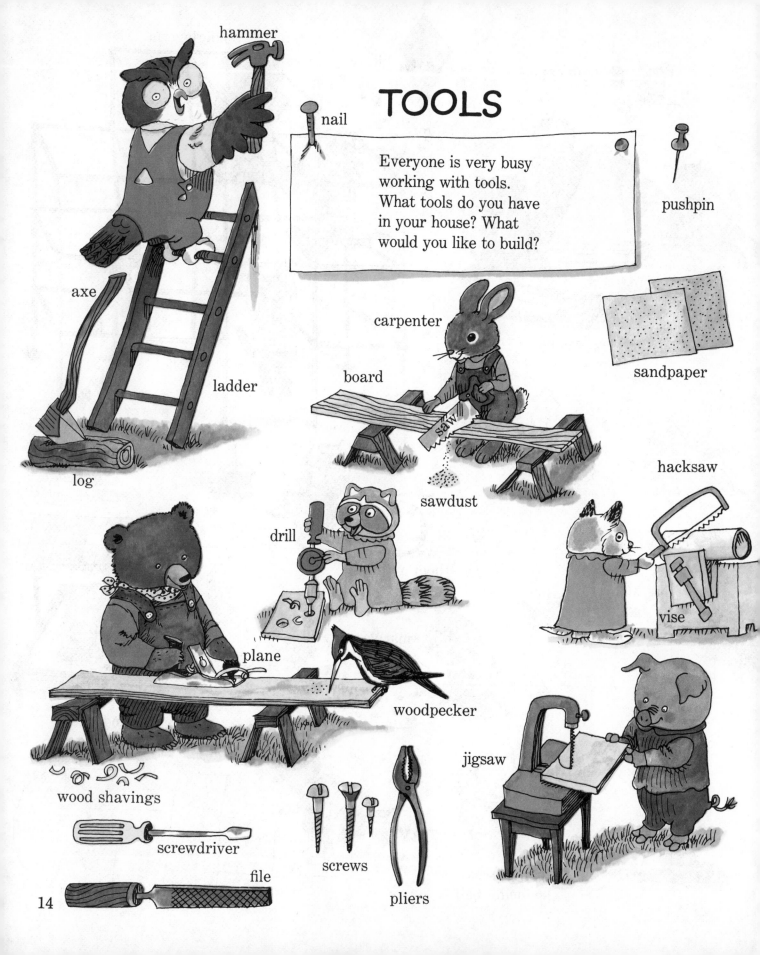

nail

TOOLS

Everyone is very busy
working with tools.
What tools do you have
in your house? What
would you like to build?

pushpin

axe

carpenter

sandpaper

board

ladder

saw

hacksaw

log

sawdust

drill

vise

plane

woodpecker

jigsaw

wood shavings

screwdriver

screws

file

pliers

14

bucksaw

trowel

bricklayer

hoe

brick wall

cement

brick

lumber

fence painter

paintbrush

ball of twine

sawhorse

barrel

paint

tack

tack hammer

hatchet

ruler

folding ruler

jackknife

toolbox

square

putty knife

shovel

bolt

nut

dirt

monkey wrench

compass

wheelbarrow

pickaxe

glue

15

crow

scarecrow

weather vane

silo

disc harrow

field

tractor

barn

hayloft

goat

stall

tin can

milk can

pail

farm truck

wagon

hen

rooster

baby chick

pigsty

Kathy Bear is going
to feed the pig.

corncrib

16

haystack

cow

apple tree

farmhouse

water pump

meadow

fence

sheep

horse

apple

grass

clothesline

clothes basket

THE BEARS' FARM

Kenny Bear is going to feed the chickens.

The Bears are working hard on their farm. What are they all doing? What is the duck doing? What is the scarecrow supposed to be doing? He is not doing it, is he?

chicken coop

mailbox

well

duck pond

duck

ducklings

bee

pitchfork

beehive

17

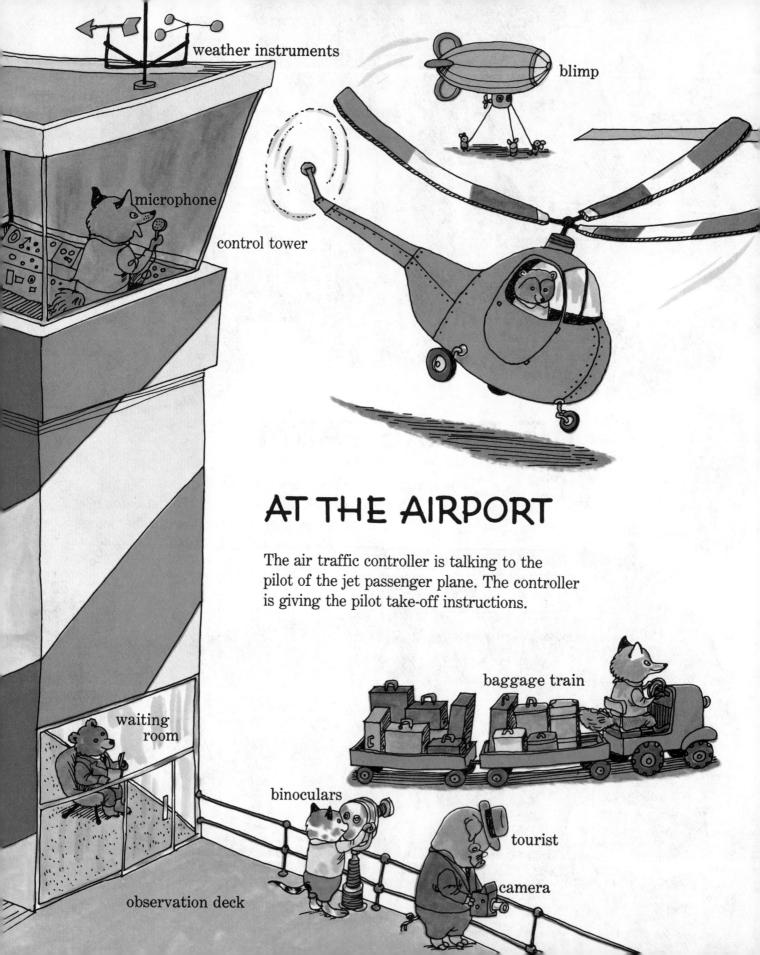

weather instruments

blimp

microphone

control tower

AT THE AIRPORT

The air traffic controller is talking to the
pilot of the jet passenger plane. The controller
is giving the pilot take-off instructions.

baggage train

waiting
room

binoculars

tourist

observation deck

camera

jet plane

wind sock

runway

hangar

runway lights

light plane

propeller

mechanic

jet military plane

jet passenger plane

pilot

tail

baggage handler

cockpit

flight attendant

fuselage

wing

baggage loader

jet engine

passenger-loading stairs

19

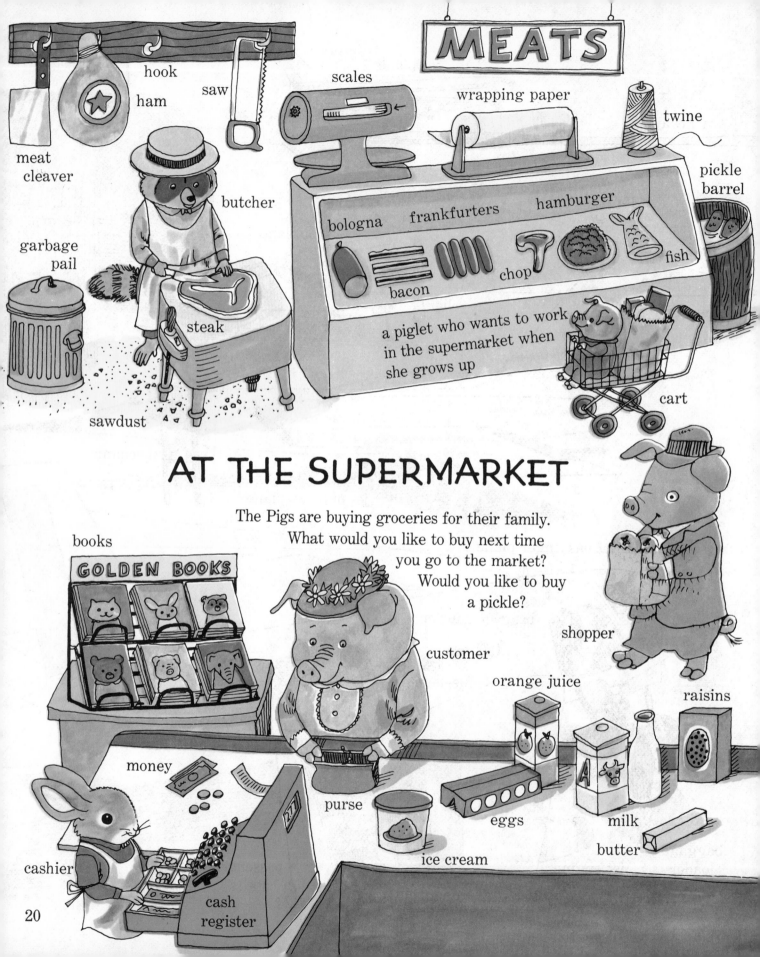

hook

ham

saw

scales

MEATS

wrapping paper

twine

meat cleaver

butcher

pickle barrel

bologna   frankfurters   hamburger

garbage pail

fish

chop

bacon

steak

a piglet who wants to work in the supermarket when she grows up

sawdust

cart

AT THE SUPERMARKET

The Pigs are buying groceries for their family.
What would you like to buy next time
you go to the market?
Would you like to buy
a pickle?

books

GOLDEN BOOKS

shopper

customer

orange juice

raisins

money

purse

cashier

eggs

milk

butter

cash register

ice cream

20

FRUITS

pineapple
bananas
scales
grocer
apples
oranges
pears
grapefruit
melons
grapes
lemons
cherries
strawberries
raspberries
blueberries
plums

VEGETABLES

corn
beans
lettuce
tomatoes
peas
spinach
potatoes
asparagus
celery
onions
beets
carrots
cucumbers
turnip

peaches
watermelon
coconut
pumpkin
cabbage
squash
cauliflower

broom

cookies
sugar
cereal
spaghetti
canned food
peanut butter
cheese
salt
apricots
baby food
bread
jam

MEALTIME

The Pig Family is having a special holiday meal. There is so much good food to enjoy! What do you see on the table that you like to eat?

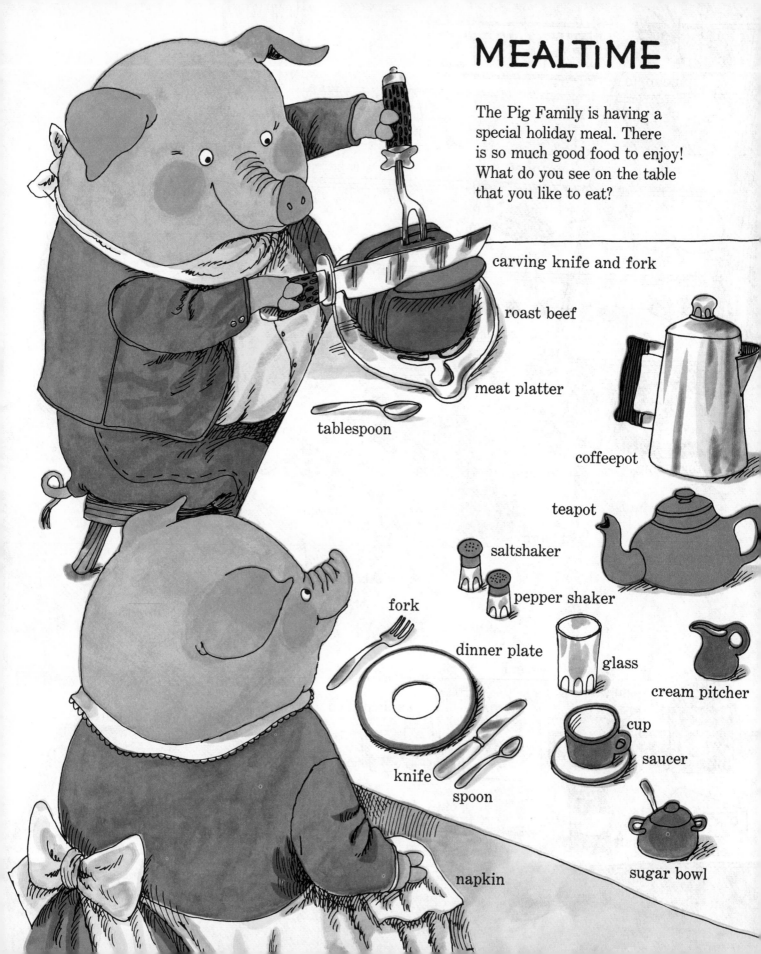

carving knife and fork

roast beef

meat platter

tablespoon

coffeepot

teapot

saltshaker

pepper shaker

fork

dinner plate

glass

cream pitcher

cup

saucer

knife

spoon

sugar bowl

napkin

turkey

cake

milk pitcher

squash

baked potatoes

green beans

gelatine

cranberry sauce

mashed potatoes

beets

onions

ice cream

peas

steak

butter

soup

pie

salad

rye bread

white bread

rolls

smokestack

submarine

stern

bow

ocean liner

police boat

tugboat

barge

POLICE

ferryboat

pirate ship

BOATS AND SHIPS

One of the things in the water is not a
boat, but it helps boats find the place they
want to go. Do you know what it is?

motorboat

paddle

canoe

24

kayak

oar rowboat

freighter

lightship

AMBROSE

coast guard ship

CG-7

oil tanker

fireboat

F.D.

fishing nets

sport-fishing boat

fishing trawler

speedboat

houseboat

raft

THE WHITE SWAN

sailboat

light buoy

25

KEEPING HEALTHY

Your doctors and your dentist are your good friends. They want you to stay healthy and strong. Will you give your doctors and dentist a big smile the next time you see them? How big a smile can you smile?

gauze bandage

adhesive tape

thermometer

stethoscope

cotton balls

tweezers

plastic bandage
for small cuts
and hurts

scissors

pills

flashlight

aspirin

medicine

rubber hammer
to make legs kick

tongue depressor
for looking down throats

eye chart

toothpaste

toothbrush

tooth

tooth
with a cavity

record chart
to show where any
cavities have been found

dental tools

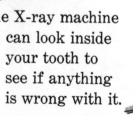
The X-ray machine
can look inside
your tooth to
see if anything
is wrong with it.

The doctor listens to your heart.

eye doctor

The eye doctor tests your eyes.

scales

hurt tail

doctor

patient

dental engine

dentist

inse bowl

instrument table

water cup

dental unit

dentist's chair

dental hygienist

The dentist looks for cavities and the dental hygienist explains how to care for your teeth.

THE BEAR TWINS GET DRESSED

Kenny Bear awakens one cold, frosty morning.
He wants to dress very warmly before
going outside.

He yawns and gets up out of bed.
He takes off his pajamas, folds
them, and puts them in a dresser
drawer.

What should he wear today to keep warm?

pajama
top

pajama
bottom

slippers

cap

He puts on his   T-shirt   undershorts   shirt   pants   overalls

necktie   sweater   socks   hat   sneakers   gloves

muffler

jacket   overcoat   raincoat   and rainhat.

As Kenny is walking out of the front
door his father says, "Don't forget
to put your boots on!"

boots

Kathy Bear stretches hard before she gets out of bed. She takes off her nightgown and hangs it on the hook in her closet.

What do you think Kathy should wear today to keep warm?

nightgown

She puts on her

underpants

undershirt

hair ribbon

blouse

skirt

sweater

kneesocks

ear muffs

shoes

snowsuit

and mittens.

She puts her change purse

into her backpack.

As Kathy is walking out of the front door her mother says, "Don't forget to put your boots on!"

Do you ever forget to put on your boots?

deer

lion

elephant

panda

monkeys

tiger

brown bear

gorilla

polar bear

30

buffalo

camel

zebra

zookeeper

giraffe

leopard

sea lion

zoo train

The veterinarian makes sure all the animals are healthy.

AT THE ZOO

Mr. and Mrs. Mouse took their children to the zoo. How will those children ever be able to get all those balloons into their house tonight? Which is your favorite animal at the zoo?

rhinoceros

balloon seller

hippopotamus

BOOK PUBLISHER

COSTUMES

skyscraper

antenna

water tank

church

NEWSPAPER OFFICE

Dancing School

traffic light

Bookstore

apartment house

DRUGSTORE

telephone booth

mailbox

book reader

mail truck

letter carrier

street

IN THE CITY

Mouse has just bought a book at the bookstore.
She is going to buy a newspaper and then join
her rabbit friends at the sidewalk cafe and drink some
lemonade with them. Show with your finger the way
she will go. Remember to have her look both
ways before she crosses a street.

fire hydrant

32

hotel

street sign

park

park
bench

statue

manhole

RESTAURANT

sidewalk cafe

barbershop

delivery
cycle

traffic
officer

DANGER

one
way

taxi

police car

THEATER

NOW PLAYING

TAXI
STAND

SUBWAY

BUS
STOP

bus

sidewalk

token seller

subway entrance

newspapers

newsstand

subway
station

33

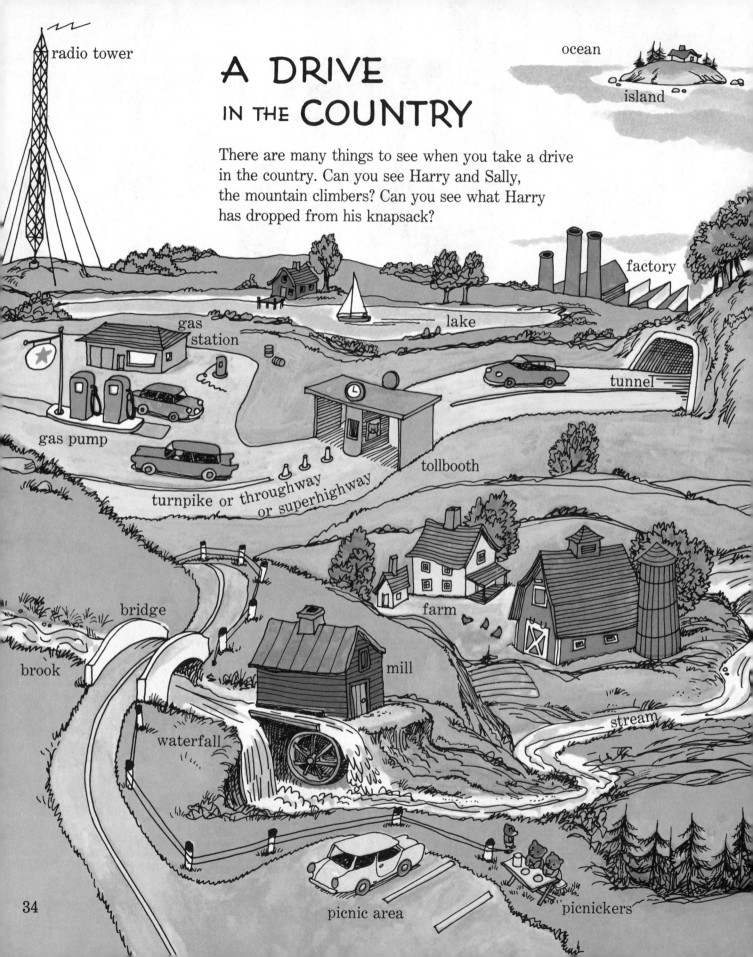

A DRIVE
IN THE COUNTRY

There are many things to see when you take a drive in the country. Can you see Harry and Sally, the mountain climbers? Can you see what Harry has dropped from his knapsack?

radio tower

ocean

island

factory

gas station

lake

tunnel

gas pump

tollbooth

turnpike or throughway or superhighway

bridge

farm

brook

mill

stream

waterfall

picnic area

picnickers

lighthouse

beach

fire lookout tower

bay

crane

woods

drawbridge

seaport

hill

tug

mountain

village

windmill

river

pond

log cabin

mountain
climbers

road

forest

knapsack

cliff

apple 35

HOLIDAYS

Holidays are happy times, aren't they?
Which holiday do you like best?
I bet you like them all.

On holidays we visit friends and relatives.
Sometimes we give or get presents.
What would you like to get for your birthday?

horn

New Year's Day

valentine

St. Valentine's Day

Easter

Easter egg

Easter bunny

Easter chick

balloons

rattle

cake

ice cream

Birthday

National Holiday

bugle

fireworks

flag

bass drum

drum

fife

uniform

36

ghost

Halloween

moon

skeleton

witch

black cat

witch's broom

pumpkin

Chanukah

trick-or-treat bag

angel

menorah

candle

Christmas

wreath

Christmas
tree

holly

ornaments

stockings

tree
lights

beard

fireplace

bag

Santa Claus

present

37

AT SCHOOL

School is fun. There are so many things we learn to do. Kathy Bear is learning how to find a lost mitten.

pencil sharpener

pencil

fountain pen

ball-point pen

paper

chalk

notebook

straw

ink

chalkboard eraser

eraser

milk

cookies

scissors

string

yarn

paper clip

paste

workbook

storybook

thumbtacks

modelling clay

lost-clothing drawer

flag

clock

bell

calendar

JANUARY

teacher

chalkboard

a b c

cat dog

map

map stand

inkwell

wastebasket

pupil

artist

desk

classroom

paper shapes

music teacher

refrigerator

kitchen cabinet

doorknob

can opener

soap

teapot

electrical outlet

counter

freezer

garbage pail

washing machine

dishwasher

laundry basket

Father Pig

eggbeater

eggshell

stool

Annie Pig

mixing bowl

batter spoon

measuring cup

rolling pin

Susan Pig

cookie cutter

dough

Peter Pig

strainer

funnel

cake pan

cookie tray

spatula

ketchup bottle

food grinder

flour bin

40

sugar bowl

mustard jar

closet

feather duster

broom

dustpan

mop

flyswatter

shelf

egg timer

Mother Pig

hood

coffeepot

teakettle

burner

vacuum cleaner

oven

stove

iron

ironing board

IN THE KITCHEN

All the Pigs like to work in the kitchen.
They are making good things to eat.
What is Father Pig making? What is
Mother Pig putting into the oven?

pestle

toaster

teaspoon

tablespoon

soup spoon

double boiler

blender

mortar

saucepan

corkscrew

ladle

colander

cutting board

measuring spoons

matches

potato masher

saltshaker

pepper grinder

electric mixer

cookbook

carving fork and knife

WHEN YOU GROW UP

What would you like to be when you are
bigger? Would you like to be a good
cook like your father? Would you like
to be a doctor or a nurse?

What would you like to be?

police officer

fire fighter

sailor

nurse

taxi driver

farmer

gardener

doctor

carpenter

musician

scientist

baker

dentist

secretary

good cook

42

singer

artist

pilot

fisherman

truck driver

teacher

garage mechanic

judge

reporter

photographer

storekeeper

librarian

dancer

daddy

mommy

THINGS WE DO

There are many things
that we can do. And there
are some things we cannot do.
What is one thing we can't do?
Look and see.

dig

blow

build

break

sleep

awaken

walk

run

stand

sit

read

watch

draw and write

44

pull

push

kick

talk

listen

shout

whisper

eat

laugh

smile

cry

drink

jump over

crawl under

fall down

we can't fly

peek

tip a hat

go up

go down

go in

come out

WORK MACHINES

Busy, busy, busy bears. Most of the bears are busy moving dirt with their machines. But there is one bear who has a machine which does something else to the dirt. Which bear is it? What is she doing?

bulldozer

dirt

shovel

dump trailer

tractor scraper

dump truck

tractor shovel

bucket loader

dirt

roller

and tractor

smooth dirt

47

rough dirt

automobile carrier

gasoline truck

GASOLINE

milk truck

A

broken-down car

tow truck

motorcycle

taxi

TAXI

sports car

48

GoldenWings Freight Line

trailer truck

SANITATION ENGINEER

garbage truck

boat trailer

CARS AND TRUCKS

Down the street go the
cars and trucks.
But look! Some of the
cars don't have drivers.
Which cars have no drivers?

station wagon

motor scooter

antique car

SCHOOL BUS

school bus

round

square

triangle

diamond

star

crescent

heart

straight

curved

cone

SHAPES AND SIZES

thin

tall

big

fat

short

little

tiny

long

short

THE BABY

father

mother

grandmother

The Cat family has a new baby kitten.
They don't know what to name it.
What would you like
to name the new baby?
Write the kitten's name here.

___ ___ ___ ___ ___ ___

uncle

bottle

baby

brother

aunt

grandfather

rattle

sister

diaper

playpen

cousin

high chair

crib

stroller

bassinet

play table

walker

baby carriage

AT THE CIRCUS

The band is playing and the animals
are doing their acts. What do you like to
watch best at the circus?

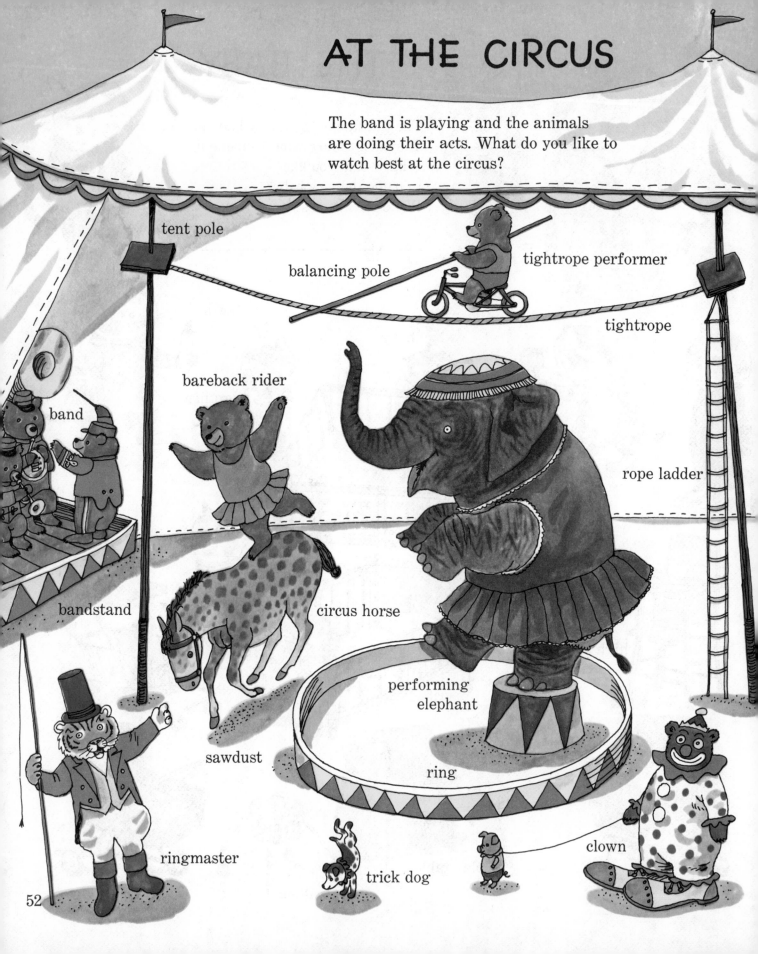

tent pole

balancing pole

tightrope performer

tightrope

bareback rider

band

rope ladder

bandstand

circus horse

performing
elephant

sawdust

ring

ringmaster

trick dog

clown

pennant

circus tent

trapeze

trapeze artist

safety net

acrobat

ticket seller

hoop

lion

whip

cage

lion tamer

trained sea lion

popcorn seller

balloon seller

juggler

53

THE FIRE FIGHTERS TO THE RESCUE

Will the brave fire fighters
put out the fire in time?
I think so, don't you?

rescue truck

POLICE

police car

nozzle

rear-wheel steerer

fire engine

hook-and-ladder
truck

hose

ladder

front-wheel
steerer

boots

helmet

first-aid kit

hook

bell

fire alarm box

bell

whistle

7

TRAINS

steam locomotive and tender

boxcar

Which train do you think
would be the most fun to run?
Would it be a freight train
or a passenger train?

signal tower

lantern

handcar

caboose

flatcar

dining car

railroad station

platform

conductor

baggage wagon

freight train

bumper

tracks

piggyback car

tank car

gondola car

switch

railroad track

ties

coal

horn

coal car

diesel switcher

passenger train

diesel streamliner

coach

crossing gate

rail

spike

711

AT THE BEACH

In the summertime it is fun
to go to the beach.
What do you think
Rabbit hears in the seashell?
Is it the sound of the waves?

telescope

lighthouse

summer cottage

oar

anchor

beach toy

shovel

rowboat

sandpiper

sand castle

waves

skate

bluefish

oyster

lobster

sea purse

scallop

hermit crab

clam

MAKING THINGS GROW

Everyone is working in the garden.
Mr. Crow has a seed in his mouth.
Do you think he will plant it?
Or will he eat it?

faucet

nozzle

hose

cornstalk

gardener

string

spade

hoe

seed row

tomato plants

seeds

seedlings

ear of corn

handle

rake

BEETS

TOMATOES

stake

stones

garden fork

fertilizer cart

THE WEATHER

When we go outdoors we see what the weather is like. Sometimes it is sunny. Sometimes it is cloudy. It can be windy, or cold, or hot. It can be snowing or raining. What was the weather like outdoors today? What is your favorite kind of weather?

sun

cloud

lightning

rain

hailstones

snowflakes

thermometer

rainbow

windmill

wind

hat

raindrops

foxtail grass

toad

toadstool

ladybug

a cat chasing a hat

puddle

mud

61

kite

rain shower

plow

robin

buds

nest

SPRING

Look at that baby lamb hop!
It is spring. She is happy.
Look at Mr. Bear coming out of
his cave! It is spring. He is happy.
Now he can use his new
lawn mower.

tree

lamb

bush

bridge

brook

fern

turtle

roots

cave

pussy willow

spring peeper

daffodil

lawn mower

crocus

violets

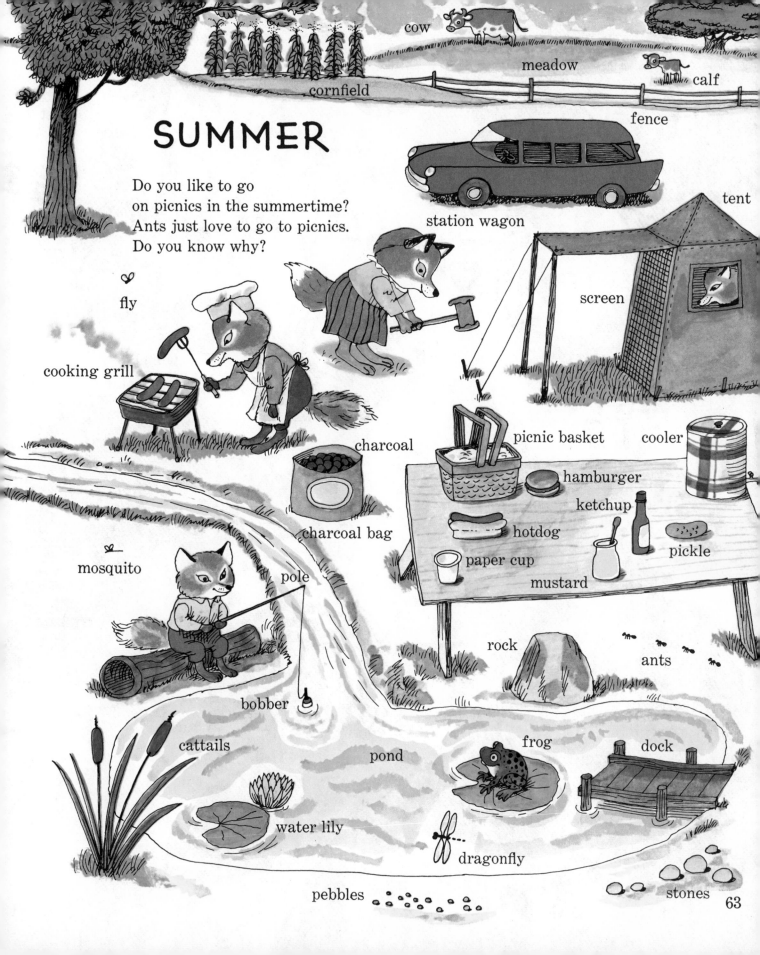

cow

meadow

calf

cornfield

fence

SUMMER

Do you like to go
on picnics in the summertime?
Ants just love to go to picnics.
Do you know why?

station wagon

tent

screen

fly

cooking grill

charcoal

picnic basket

cooler

hamburger

ketchup

charcoal bag

hotdog

paper cup

pickle

mosquito

pole

mustard

rock

ants

bobber

cattails

frog

dock

pond

water lily

dragonfly

pebbles

stones

63

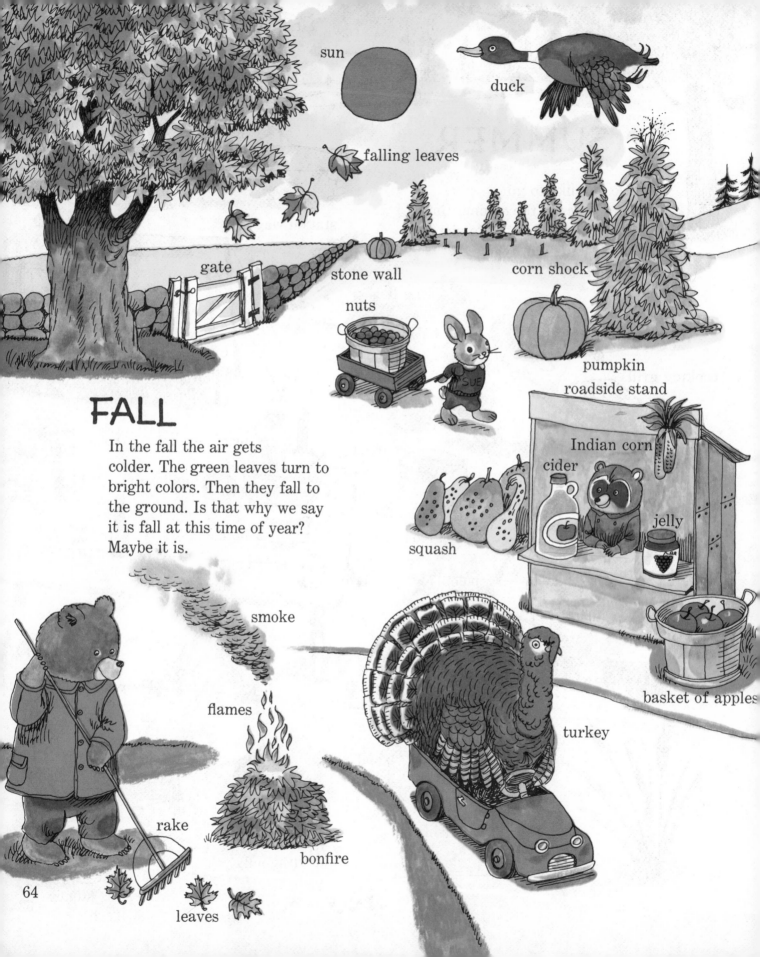

sun

duck

falling leaves

gate

stone wall

corn shock

nuts

pumpkin

roadside stand

Indian corn

cider

jelly

squash

FALL

In the fall the air gets colder. The green leaves turn to bright colors. Then they fall to the ground. Is that why we say it is fall at this time of year? Maybe it is.

smoke

flames

rake

bonfire

turkey

basket of apples

leaves

64

snowstorm

WINTER

There are many ways to
have fun on the snow and ice.
Maybe you would like to do
all of them. Would you?

sleigh

icicle

fishing
shack

skis

sled

toboggan

ice fishing

snow

ice-skating rink

ice skater

snowball

hockey stick

puck

muffler

ice skates

spare tire

pipe

jeep

snowplow

snowman

a pig all wrapped up

65

LITTLE THINGS

Here are many little things.
What little thing do you sometimes
put on your bedroom wall?

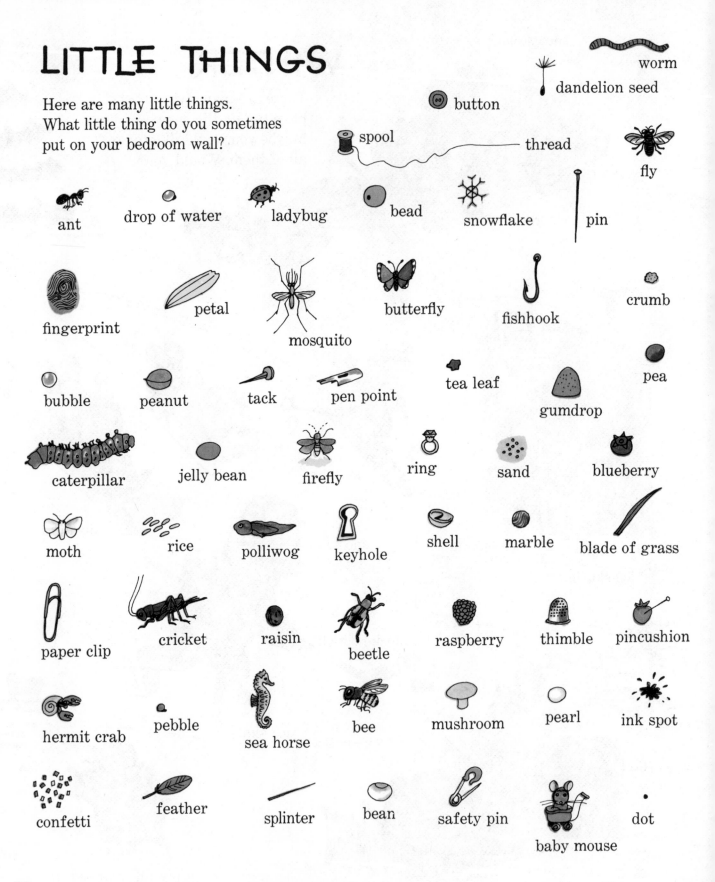

worm

dandelion seed

button

spool

thread

fly

ant

drop of water

ladybug

bead

snowflake

pin

fingerprint

petal

mosquito

butterfly

fishhook

crumb

bubble

peanut

tack

pen point

tea leaf

gumdrop

pea

caterpillar

jelly bean

firefly

ring

sand

blueberry

moth

rice

polliwog

keyhole

shell

marble

blade of grass

paper clip

cricket

raisin

beetle

raspberry

thimble

pincushion

hermit crab

pebble

sea horse

bee

mushroom

pearl

ink spot

confetti

feather

splinter

bean

safety pin

dot

baby mouse

PARTS OF THE BODY

Bears use their paws to pick things up.
What do you use?

ear

hair

head

eye

cheek

nose

mouth

tongue

tooth

lips

neck

shoulder

chest

back

arm

elbow

stomach

waist

wrist

claw or finger

paw or hand

hip

thigh

bottom (try not to be
spanked here)

leg

knee

claw or toe

heel

foot

BEDTIME

Little Elephant is getting ready for bed.
But who is that hiding under the bed?
Find that rascal and tell her to brush her
teeth and get ready for bed, too.

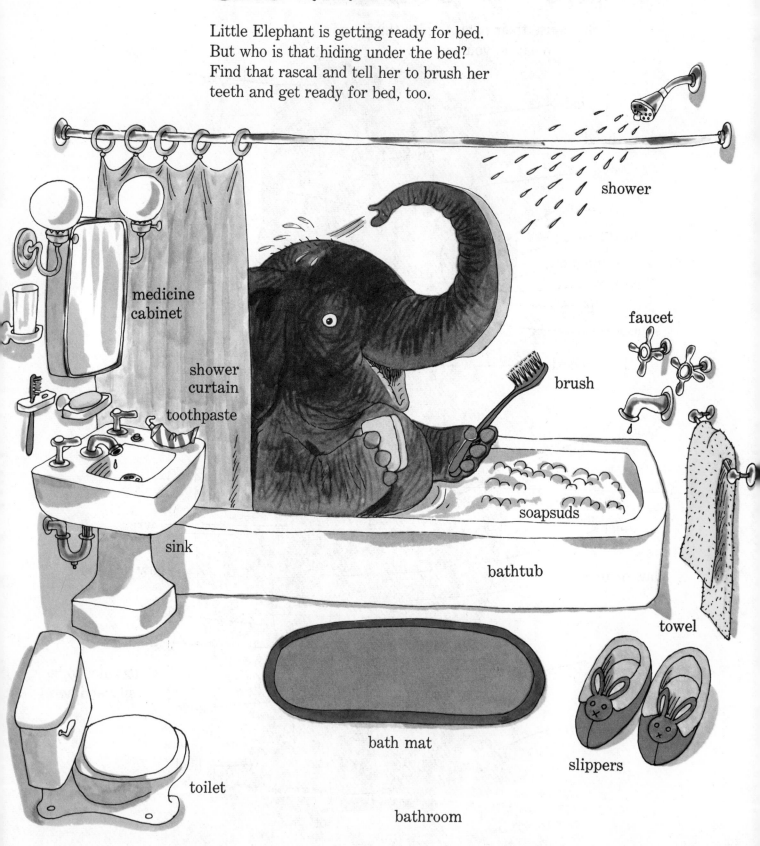

shower

medicine
cabinet

faucet

shower
curtain

brush

toothpaste

soapsuds

sink

bathtub

towel

bath mat

slippers

toilet

bathroom

ceiling

wall

picture hook

Mommy

moon

stars

picture

book

pillow

toy friend

blanket

sheet

hole

chest

bed

bedroom

rug

69

NUMBERS

How high can you count?
Can you count up to
twenty ladybugs?
I'll bet you can.

1 one whale

2 two walruses

3 three piggy banks

4 four bells

5 five grasshoppers

6 six eggs

7	seven caterpillars
8	eight spools
9	nine spiders
10	ten keys
11	eleven ants
12	twelve rings
13	thirteen gumdrops
14	fourteen leaves
15	fifteen snowflakes
16	sixteen acorns
17	seventeen pins
18	eighteen buttons
19	nineteen beads
20	twenty ladybugs

1

Do you know a 6–13 year old who would like to receive free information on the Young Model Builders Club?

This club offers a wide selection of model kits to assemble, including airplanes, military vehicles, drag racers, helicopters, vans, and more.

To receive free information on this exciting club and to find out how to receive a free model kit, please write:

YOUNG MODEL
BUILDERS CLUB
Dept. 83Z03
P.O. Box 10265
Des Moines, IA 50336

Offer available in the U.S. only.